Contents

Any words appearing in the text in bold, **like this**, are explained in the glossary. You can also look out for them in the Word bank at the bottom of each page.

Hard lessons to learn

Over 100 years ago only very rich people would have been able to send their children to school. But in the 1900s many countries made education free for all pupils. Children then had to attend school by law.

The scrape of chalk on a blackboard, the clang of a bell in the playground, the swish of a **cane** . . . through history these sounds have sent shivers down the spines of many schoolchildren. For many young people, their school days were not just scary. They were terrible, cruel, and often painful. Some pupils still say they hate learning at school. But if they could swap places with someone from the past, they would see that school today is not quite so bad after all!

If you did not go to school, you faced a lifetime of hard and poorly-paid work, like these boys who sorted coal all day long.

Many teachers believed that hitting students stopped them from growing up to be badly behaved.

　Word bank　　cane　stick used to beat students as punishment

Painful punishments

Until quite recently, schools used harsh punishments on pupils who misbehaved or did not work hard enough. These punishments often included:

- being hit with a belt
- having a wooden cane whacked across the back of the legs
- having a ruler cracked down across the knuckles
- being hit on the bottom with a bunch of birch twigs.

These punishments were given for all sorts of reasons, like spelling a word incorrectly, not finishing homework on time, or talking in class.

Find out later...

Why did you once have to carry logs to school?

Why would you have to wear a pointed hat?

When was homework banned?

Education in the past

Just over a hundred years ago, most people in the world could not read. Only those who could afford books and an education were taught to read and write. These people would get all the important jobs because they had these skills. People who could read held all the power in society. That was the way it was for thousands of years.

Ancient Egypt

Learning to read in ancient Egypt was hard work. This was because there were no letters. Instead they used pictures called **hieroglyphs** as symbols for different words or sounds. Only a few rich boys learnt to read. They would then become **scribes**, who were seen as very important people.

Painful advice

A father in ancient Egypt warned his son that school was not meant to be enjoyable:

"PASS NO DAY BEING IDLE OR YOU WILL BE BEATEN. THE EAR OF A BOY IS ON HIS BACK. HE LISTENS BEST WHEN HE IS BEATEN."

– Amenemope, an ancient Egyptian scribe.

Ancient Egyptian scribes.

Word bank   **hieroglyphics**   system of writing mainly in pictures, like scripts of the ancient Egyptians

Ancient China

In ancient China only a few children learned to read. This was difficult to do as Chinese writing is made up of many different shapes, marks, and lines, and there are hundreds of letters to learn. Over 2,000 years ago there were no paper or pens. Words were scratched onto turtle shells and animal bones before the first paper and writing brushes were used.

Only the sons of leaders and chief soldiers would have gone to school to learn to read. They had to work very hard, because nobody got a powerful job without being able to write.

Chinese writing is difficult to learn.

Imagine doing your homework in Egyptian hieroglyphics!

First big schools

The Chinese Emperor Wudi started a system of schools over 2,100 years ago in China. Only boys were allowed to go to these schools. The Grand School began with only a few boys but, after 100 years, it had over 30,000 students.

idle lazy and not active
scribe person who studies, writes, or copies scripts

Ancient learning

In ancient Rome it was just boys who learned to read and write. But that was only if their fathers could teach them. Fathers also taught their sons about Roman law, their gods, history, and about being a good soldier. Girls were taught by their mothers to spin, weave, and sew.

Some older boys learned **Latin** in their teachers' homes. They had to arrive very early each morning before the sun rose, so they carried candles to light the way. Education was not meant to be pleasant, and beatings with an eel-skin strap were thought to do boys good!

Romans

Roman books were **scrolls** made of animal skins. Children learning to write had to scratch letters into wax spread on wooden boards. The few who went to school spent a lot of time learning long speeches by heart. This was to get important ideas stuck in their minds.

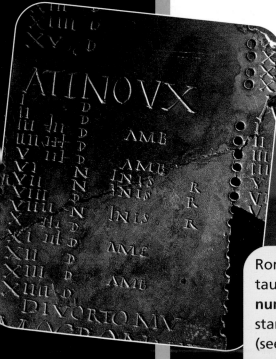

A Roman boy scratches writing on to a wax tablet. The surface of the wax could be scraped clean and re-used.

Roman sums were taught using **Roman numerals**. Each letter stands for a number (see page 45).

Roman numerals   ancient Roman way of writing numbers using letters

Greeks

Even earlier than the Romans, the ancient Greeks had also had strict ideas about education. Only rich Greek boys went to school. They started at seven years old, and stayed until they were fifteen. They had to learn poems by heart. This was partly because books were very expensive and rare. If they did not learn well enough, the boys were beaten with sticks. They were also taught to fight like soldiers.

Greek girls were not allowed to go to school. They stayed at home and were taught to cook and weave. Some girls even learned to read and write at home.

The ancient Greek philosopher Homer. He wrote huge poems about the world and history.

Tough subject

The ancient Greeks were very keen on learning about the world, working out how we think, and discovering the meaning behind everything. This was called **philosophy**. Rich boys as young as seven had to study this at school and write all about it.

scroll   roll of material that has been prepared as a writing surface
philosophy   study of ideas, meaning, truth, right and wrong

The Middle Ages

The time in Europe from about AD 500 to 1500 was called the **Middle Ages,** or Medieval Europe. During this time the Roman Catholic Church was growing in power and building churches in many countries. Some men who joined the church became **monks** and went to live in buildings called **monasteries.** They studied in these buildings and also taught children how to read and write.

Women who became **nuns** lived in **convents,** where they would also teach the children whose parents could afford to pay for lessons. Classes were very strict, with no fun allowed.

Early writing

There were very few schools in Europe 1,000 years ago. No **peasant** child would be able to read. Young men who trained to be monks would learn how to write out parts of the Bible in Latin. But any mistake would be punished – with pain!

The detailed work of a monk from AD 1200.

bishop leader in the Christian church
peasant poor person or farm worker

Careful what you say...

Nuns taught girls how to do spinning and needlework. They also made them learn prayers by saying them over and over again.

Boys would attend monasteries between the ages of seven and fourteen. In England all the lessons were taught in **Latin**. If a boy was caught speaking in English, he would be hit with a rod – one strike for every English word spoken. A similar punishment would be used if a boy was late to school, or if he made a mistake with his work.

Young monks being taught at a monastery around AD 600.

Old school

Winchester College in England was built over 620 years ago, and is one of the oldest schools still in use today (below). The **Bishop** of Winchester started the school in 1382 to teach "70 poor and needy **scholars**.". Today the school is far bigger – and its fees are also far higher!

---

scholar   someone who attends a school or studies under a teacher

There were still very few schools anywhere in the world 500 years ago. Only a few wealthy people could afford to send their children to school. Most young people had to work, earning money for the family to survive.

North America

Until the first Europeans settled in North America in the 16th century, the land was **inhabited** by hundreds of Native American groups who spoke over 250 languages. Young people were often taught by their parents or group leaders. The Iroquois tribe thought that children should be carefully looked after. They said, "a child's life is as thin as a leaf." **Corporal punishment** was rare because of this, and children learnt through exciting stories about animals and nature.

No reading

For thousands of years learning and knowledge was passed down from parents to children through storytelling. This was all done from memory, without the use of books. This was how Native Americans taught their children about their three most important subjects:

- survival
- the spirits
- right and wrong.

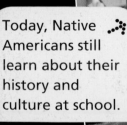

Today, Native Americans still learn about their history and culture at school.

Word bank

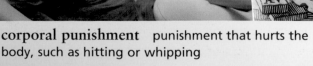

corporal punishment punishment that hurts the body, such as hitting or whipping

Europe

Johann Gutenberg invented the printing press in Germany in the 1450s. This made it possible to make many copies of any book. William Caxton printed the first book in English in 1475, and by the 1500s books were being printed all over Europe. Even so, few schools could afford books at this time.

Even by 1600 very few children attended school, so only a few people were reading the books being printed. About 72 percent of men and 92 percent of women in Britain could not sign their own names at this time. It took years before ordinary people got to even see books, let alone read them.

Christ Church College, Oxford University, opened in 1546.

ABRAHAM VON WERDT.

Printing presses were huge pieces of machinery when they were first invented. It took at least two people to operate just one press.

University

At the end of the Middle Ages more advanced schools started to be built in Europe. They were called **universities**, and some fourteen and fifteen-year-old students were able to study there. The most important were at Paris in France, Oxford and Cambridge in England, and Bologna in Italy. Girls were not allowed to attend.

university   place for learning different subjects, passing exams, and gaining qualifications

The first English settlers arrived in North America in the 1620s. They set up home on the east coast and called it New England. They built the first schools here. The Boston Latin School opened in 1635, and is thought to have been the first town school of North America. These schools had strict rules and children had to learn parts of the Bible by heart each day.

Any men who could read and write were allowed to teach, as long as they were members of a church and kept out of trouble. These teachers were sometimes paid with cows, pigs, corn, or apples!

Reading boards

Throughout the 1600s schools had very little paper or books. Children learned to read from a hornbook. This was a piece of wood that had the alphabet written on it. It was covered with a thin, clear layer of animal horn to protect it.

Pilgrim children in a lesson in the late 1600s.

Hornbooks were used to teach basic reading.

Word bank   quill   pen made from a feather

School life

In winter children had to carry firewood to school. It was burned in the fireplace to warm the classroom. Any pupils who did not bring any wood had to sit furthest from the fireplace in the cold!

Boys learned to write by copying out Bible texts. They wrote lines like "the **idle** fool is whipped at school" to remind them to work hard. Some words were spelt differently, and there were no strict rules about how to spell. A teacher in the 1600s in New England wrote that he taught "writeing and spilling."

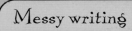

Messy writing

Pupils in the 1600s used **quill** pens made from goose feathers (above). The teacher made the ink for children to dip their quills into. Ink often smudged, so they sprinkled pounce across the page. Pounce was a powder like sand that soaked up wet ink.

Hard times

In most countries in the 1700s there were no laws to make children go to school. Such laws were not passed until the late 1800s. Until then, many young people had no education at all. Parents had to pay if they wanted their children to go to school and most families were far too poor to afford this. They sent their children to work in mines, mills, and factories instead.

Schools were run in the belief that learning had to be hard work with no fun. Many teachers believed strongly that children should be seen and not heard. Anyone making the slightest sound would be punished.

Teaching poor children

Not all adults believed in treating children harshly. A famous English preacher, George Whitefield (above), who lived from 1714 to 1770, went to North America and set up a school for **orphans** in Georgia. He wrote:

"29 January, 1740. Took in three orphans, the most pitiful objects, I think, I ever saw... They have been used to hard labour. . . and treated in a terrible manner."

"You will do as you are told!" ⋯▸

Word bank   orphan   young person whose parents have died

Scary lessons

Teachers often used fear to make children do as they were told. Beatings were common. If anyone spoke or giggled while the teacher was talking, the teacher would lash out with a birch **cane** or a stick with a hard little ball on the end of it. This whacked the pupil across the head.

In the early 1700s, some people thought that girls did not need to read because they did not do "important jobs". Instead, some richer parents sent their girls to teachers to learn how to sing, sew, and to carry out polite conversation.

By the 1750s, more people were reading in parts of New England than anywhere else in the world. One reason was that the children in this new land needed to read the Bible for guidance. Up to 75 percent of boys could read many words by themselves. More girls were getting the chance, too, with about 65 percent of them gaining basic reading skills.

Rich and poor

By the 1800s the world was developing fast. Europe and the United States were getting richer from the growth in industry. But the gap between the rich factory owners and the poor factory workers grew wider. Poor children had to work all day in factories, while the rich could afford a good education.

Divided classes

Young people were either rich and educated, or poor and uneducated. Rich children were often taught at home by a **governess** or a master. Then, by the time they were eight years old, many boys would be sent away to live in **boarding schools**.

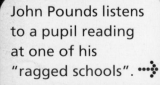

John Pounds listens to a pupil reading at one of his "ragged schools".

Word bank   **boarding school**   school where most of the pupils live during the school term

Country schools

Just over 150 years ago most schools in **rural** North America were closed for many months of the year. Since many children helped out on farms, school did not start until November when the harvest was over. Older boys often missed school in the spring and summer because of farm work.

Most schools only had one classroom, so students of all different ages were taught in the same class. They were grouped by the books they could read, not by their age. Some teachers were only in their late teens.

A teacher in the house

In parts of the United States rich children had private tutors to visit their homes. In poorer areas a travelling teacher might come to stay for a while. This was because most teachers were not paid well. Some of them even had to live with their students.

Richer children were often taught at home by a private teacher. ⁖⋯

governess   woman who teaches and trains a child in a private home

City slums

Cities across the United States and Europe grew quickly as more factories were built. People from rural areas rushed to the cities to find work. The **Industrial Revolution** spread through the United States in the 1800s. But there were never enough houses, so workers crowded into poor **slum** areas. Diseases and crime spread quickly. Something had to be done. Many leaders believed the only answer to these growing problems was a good education.

Schools began to be built in cities in the mid-1800s in the hope of giving poorer children the chance to learn. Even so, some people felt it was dangerous to teach the poor to read and get too clever!

A different world

Throughout the 1800s rich parents continued to pay for their boys to learn **Latin**, Greek, mathematics, history, geography, and sport in **boarding schools**. Most girls in rich homes would still be taught at home by a **governess**. They would learn French, housekeeping, music, and sewing, as well as how to care for children.

A girl plays piano for her family in 1900.

Word bank   **Industrial Revolution**   time of great change and development in industry and work

More pupils

Standards of teaching and learning in the city schools were sometimes bad. Teachers often struggled to keep control of some of the unruly children. Fights were even known to break out in some classrooms.

In the United States, more laws were made to improve education:

1834 Pennsylvania becomes the first state to use **taxes** to pay for public education for more children, not just those from poor slum areas.

1852 Massachusetts passes the first law in the country to make children aged 8 to 14 attend school for at least 12 weeks each year.

Slates could be used over and over again.

Most people who moved to the cities during the Industrial Revolution lived in poor, rundown conditions.

A clean slate

Slates were like small blackboards for students to write on. They were used in schools in Europe and the United States in the 1800s, when paper was expensive. Students were supposed to clean their slates with a damp cloth but, instead, they often spat on them, and rubbed them with their sleeves!

slum   city area with dirty run-down housing, and poor living conditions

Boarding school

There were many **boarding schools** in Europe and the United States in the 1800s. Some were dreary places for poor **orphans** who had nowhere else to go. Most boarding schools were only for those who could pay the high fees. Students slept in **dormitories**, ate together in large dining rooms, and went home only in the holidays. Some students were miserable being away from home for so long. Older boys sometimes bullied younger students, forcing them to be their servants with beatings.

Public or private?

A British "public school" is what Americans call a "private school." They both charge parents to send their children to them. British schools were called "public" because they took any student who could pay, from anywhere in the country. For that reason, they were nearly always boarding schools. In the United States they are "private" because only those who pay can attend.

These girls attend a private school in Louisiana, United States.

A scene from *Tom Brown's Schooldays*. In the stories Tom Brown becomes the target of the school bully, Flashman.

dormitory   large room where several people sleep in rows of beds

Australia

In the 1800s few people in Australia could afford to send children to private boarding schools. Instead some pupils were taught by a respected local person, such as a doctor's wife.

Any pupil over the age of thirteen could apply to become a teacher and be in charge of other pupils. They did not have to have a qualification to teach as most teaching at this time just involved repeating times-tables and listing other facts.

Did you know?

The United States once had boarding schools just for young Native Americans (above). By 1899, 25 such schools were in 15 states, with a total of 20,000 students. These schools were formed to teach students how to become more like Europeans. In some cases, students were not even allowed to speak in their own Native American languages.

Over 100 years ago

School for all

In the United Kingdom from 1870 all children between five and ten years old were meant to go to school. Yet many did not attend because they still had to pay a small sum of money to go. That was too much for some families. By 1891, schools were at last made free for all children, until they left at ten years old.

From the 1850s to the early 1900s more and more children were sent to school. With growing class sizes, many schools brought in even stricter rules to control students.

Working together

In most schools all pupils had to do the same work as each other at exactly the same time. The teacher would shout a command, and all pupils would open their books together. At the second command they began copying sentences from the blackboard. Anyone who could not keep up, who did not pay attention, or who had learning problems would soon get into trouble.

A more interesting lesson from 100 years ago.

Obey

Some schools had a list of rules on the wall. These rules are reported to have come from a school in Iowa, United States, in the 1870s:

1. Respect your teacher. Obey him and accept his punishments.
2. If the teacher calls your name after class, straighten the benches, sweep the room, dust, and leave everything tidy.

Rules for teachers could be strict as well:
1. Teachers must fill oil lamps and clean chimneys.
2. Each teacher will bring a bucket of water and coal each day.
3. The teacher who performs his job without fault for 5 years will be given an increase of 14 pence per week in his pay.

– The Blackwell History of Education Museum, Illinois, United States

School drop-out

At the start of the 1900s many children in the United States dropped out of school before the age of sixteen. Instead, they went to work in factories (above), farms, and mines to earn money for their families. Those who wanted to be doctors or lawyers were the only ones who stayed on at school.

Teachers

Schools were not just scary places for pupils. Teachers could also have a hard time. In the United States, in the late 1800s, one-room schools with just one teacher would hold between 20 to 40 pupils. When **immigrants** arrived, schools had to cope with even larger numbers of students, many unable to speak English. By now girls were also attending school, but they had to sit on the other side of the room from the boys.

Teachers had little training and had to teach students of all ages. Every winter's morning, they lit the fire before the students arrived. They had to sweep the room in the evening after everyone had left – unless a student could be punished with the chore.

Keeping warm

Teachers in schools in cold parts of the United States had to keep the schoolroom warm. They had log fires, but during severe winter weather when students arrived numb with cold, the teacher kept a basin of warm water for them to dip their hands into.

Some students had to wear their hats, scarves, and coats in lessons to keep warm!

Henry Patterson (on the left) taught a huge class at Glenwood School in North Dakota, United States, 1899.

immigrant   person who comes to live permanently in a foreign country

More rules

It was not until the late 1800s that women were allowed to become teachers. Many people still did not think that women could keep pupils in order. Teachers – especially female teachers – often had to obey strict rules themselves, like these from a female teacher's contract in Sacramento, United States, in the 1900s:

1. YOU MAY NOT RIDE IN A CARRIAGE WITH ANY MAN UNLESS HE IS YOUR FATHER OR BROTHER.
2. YOU MUST WEAR AT LEAST TWO PETTICOATS.
3. YOUR DRESSES MUST BE NO SHORTER THAN 5 CENTIMETRES (2 INCHES) ABOVE THE ANKLE.

The teacher's desk

The teacher often sat at a raised desk while pupils stood around the wood burner to read out their work, like in this US country school in 1875 (below).

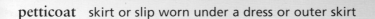

petticoat   skirt or slip worn under a dress or outer skirt

Punishment

Although some countries banned **caning** in schools in the late 1800s, the United Kingdom, United States, and Australia kept using the cane for many more years. Schools often recorded the reasons why pupils were caned in a "punishment book". Boys were usually caned across their bottoms, while girls were hit across their hands or bare legs. Here are examples of bad behaviour that resulted in caning:

- using a pea-shooter in school
- toasting bread on the stove using a ruler
- stabbing a pen into the floor
- flicking boys' ears with elastic
- writing notes to other students in class.

Some teachers broke their canes from hitting pupils so hard. Others stopped their canes from breaking by keeping them in jars of water. This made sure the canes stayed bendy.

Being shamed

Pupils who could not keep up with schoolwork had to sit in the corner of class, and wear an arm band with the word "**dunce**" written on it. They would wear a tall, cone-shaped hat with a large "D" marked on the front (below). This was supposed to shame the pupil into working harder.

Sometimes older pupils were made to hold a pupil who was to be caned.

The dunce's cap is named after John Duns Scotus, a 13th-century **philosopher**.

Word bank　**dunce**　any pupil who did not work as quickly as the teacher wanted them to

Beatings

Some teachers in the United States punished students by drawing a circle on the chalkboard and making the pupil put his or her nose on the middle of the circle. The pupil had to stand there as long as the teacher wanted.

A wooden spoon across the hand was very painful!

These punishments were given at Old Town School in San Diego, California:

- Boys and girls playing together – four **lashes**.
- Telling lies – seven lashes.
- Swearing at school – eight lashes.
- Misbehaving towards girls – ten lashes.

The punishment "Black Book"

25 February, 1878 John Nevils: given the cane for bringing a mouse into the classroom and creating a disturbance.

22 October, 1884 William Chamberlin: has been very **idle** and careless with his lessons for 2 weeks. Last night he refused to obey his teacher Miss Crosby. Ruler on each hand four times.

– From a school's Black Book in Westchester, New York, United States.

lashes beatings with a stick, whip, or cane

Unpleasant learning

Around 100 years ago very few teachers understood that people learned in different ways and at different speeds. Teaching everyone in exactly the same way was still seen as the best way to get students to learn. No one thought about the special needs of pupils who spoke a foreign language, or those who had a learning disability. School could be a cruel place for some students.

It was not surprising that some young people struggled to learn when they arrived at school shivering in the winter. If the teacher then shouted at them or beat them for not being able to remember their times-tables, life at school would have been a real misery.

A repeat dose

Many parents believed the only way to make children learn and behave was through strict **discipline**. A lot of parents would be so ashamed to hear that their child had been **caned** at school that they would give him or her another good thrashing at home (above) – just to make the lesson sink in!

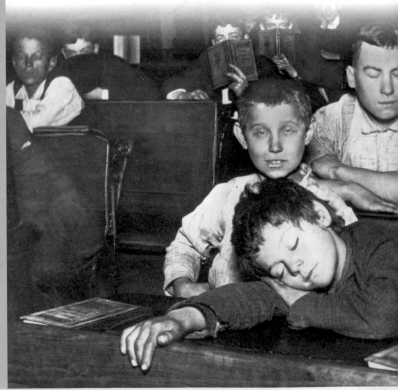

Word bank **discipline** system of rules to control behaviour

New York

There were nearly half a million school-age children in New York, United States, by the mid-1890s. The problem was that there were not enough buildings and teachers for everyone. Most schools were so overcrowded that thousands of young people had to be turned away. Some schools had to work two half-day shifts so that classrooms could be used for one set of pupils in the morning and another set in the afternoon. The buildings were often cold, damp, and falling apart, but the students still turned up because education was so important.

Another exciting lesson at a school on the Lower East Side, New York, 1886!

Maria Montessori in 1896.

Mixed-race schools

Children from different races were once kept apart in US schools. By 1880, California had passed a law to stop this. Even so, not all young people were welcome: "Children of filthy and **vicious** habits, or suffering from **infectious** diseases can be **excluded**."

Keeping apart

From the 1600s to the 1800s slaves were taken from Africa to work in fields and factories across the United States. The children of these African-American slaves were not allowed to go to school. In fact, as early as 1740, South Carolina made it illegal for slaves to learn to read. Other southern states soon followed by banning black children from all education. Even so, some were secretly taught to read the Bible.

Anyone caught teaching African Americans could be arrested and charged with a large fine. Slaves caught learning could be whipped. Despite this, some slaves did learn to read as they believed that education would lead to their freedom.

Singing hymns at school.

Students and teachers in 1865 – the year that young black people were finally allowed to go to school.

Word bank   infectious   easily spread
protest display of unwillingness or disapproval

Slave schools

When slavery finally ended in the United States in 1865, young black people were at last able to go to school. Even so, it took many years before they could go to any school and be treated fairly. Some cities had schools for black children only, keeping them apart from white children. This was called **segregation**.

"Black schools" often had less money than "white schools". As late as 1949, Clarendon County in South Carolina spent £97 on each white pupil but just £23 for each black pupil. At black schools, teachers were paid far less so the best teachers often went to the better-paid white schools.

Little Rock Nine

Less than 50 years ago segregation was still a problem in some US schools until it was banned across the country in the 1960s. In 1957 nine black students were prevented from attending Little Rock High School in Arkansas (below). This caused huge **protests** and riots, and the whole case became famous in the struggle for equal rights for black people.

segregation separating one race, class, or group from another

20th century changes

Important dates

1900: The school-leaving age in the United Kingdom was twelve years old. Most thirteen-year-olds had full-time jobs.

1917: The school-leaving age in the UK was raised from twelve to fourteen years old. All US states passed laws to provide transport to school.

1918: All US states offered free education for all students.

The 20th century saw the biggest growth in education across the world. More schools were built, more teachers were trained, and more children were taught to read and write than was ever thought possible. Whereas school was once only for wealthy people, all children had the right to an education by the end of the 1900s in many countries across the world.

There were all kinds of changes:
- Teachers began to understand how children's minds learn and develop.
- Exciting new technology was brought into classrooms.
- Many young people had opportunities they never had before.

A school leaver **apprentice** at the Dragon Paper Works in London, UK, 1915.

A group of students buy and sell stamps. The money went towards the war effort.

Word bank

disrupted thrown into disorder
evacuate remove people from a place of danger

War

Despite the improvements, millions of young people across Europe lost their education altogether due to World War 2 in the 1940s.

Children's schooldays in the 1940s were badly **disrupted**. Teachers went away to fight, there were shortages of food and clothes, and there was also the danger of bombs falling. Although there was less to fear in the United States, which was not involved in the bombing raids happening in Europe, young Americans still lost out in education. Books, paper, and teachers were suddenly in short supply.

On the move

Millions of children had to move to new homes and schools during World War 2. They were **evacuated** so they could live in safer places (above), away from the bombing raids. Sometimes all the children in a school had to move many miles away. Schools in Australia, Canada, and the United States had to take in hundreds of **refugees** from the United Kingdom.

refugee   person who flees to safety in another country, usually because of war or famine

Sweat and tears

Through the 1900s schools were expected to do far more than just teach the young to read, write, and do sums. They had to train bodies as well as minds. Young people had to learn how to be fit and healthy.

Many countries made physical training **compulsory** in schools. All students had to take part in exercises and sports each week in all weathers – often followed by a freezing wash in cold showers. The games teacher was often seen as a strict sergeant-major, putting his students through great pain!

School dinners

As early as 1906 some schools in the United Kingdom served meals to make sure hungry children were fit for lessons. Sometimes the menu was oatmeal porridge with milk and treacle, followed by bread and margarine or **dripping**.

EVERY CHILD NEEDS A GOOD SCHOOL LUNCH

THE WAR FOOD ADMINISTRATION WILL HELP YOUR COMMUNITY START A
SCHOOL LUNCH PROGRAM

Schoolgirls from the 1930s perform a gym display in their school uniforms. ⋯▸

During World War 2, the US government issued posters such as this to encourage healthy eating amongst children. ⋮▸

   compulsory   required by law to do something

Keeping fit

Today, a lot of school students are able to use the latest fitness equipment as they exercise in the school's gym. Computer printouts show fitness levels and check their progress. Around 50 years ago the most high-tech sports equipment in most schools was a bat, ball, or a hula hoop.

In the 1950s a study in the United States reported that 60 percent of young American people failed to do well at fitness tests. This caused alarm, as only 9 percent of students in Europe failed on the same tests. As a result, there was a big growth in school health and fitness programmes across the United States.

Healthy eating

In the 21st century, many countries are worried about falling levels of health and fitness in young people. There are also concerns about all the junk food being eaten. Many schools in the United Kingdom and the United States are now provided with oranges, apples, and bananas.

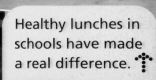

Healthy lunches in schools have made a real difference.

dripping   solid fat made from roasted meat, used in cooking or for food

When homework was banned...

In 1901 a law was made in California to ban homework for all students under the age of fifteen. In the early 1900s, many adults formed a group to get rid of all homework in schools. But things changed quickly as soon as Russia launched *Sputnik* into orbit! However, a US women's magazine called the *Ladies' Home Journal* still went on to blame homework for harming children's health.

Heaps of homework

Over 50 years ago homework was not such an important part of school life as it is today. However, the launch of a Russian **satellite** called *Sputnik* in 1957 changed all this. The United States became worried that Russia was getting ahead in science and space travel. It seemed that Russian students were learning more than US students. Something had to be done to make US schools work harder. Students would have to do more schoolwork at home to catch up.

In the 1980s and 1990s most people felt that homework helped students to progress with their studies, so younger children were given more and more homework.

Modern times

Today, many students have to do hours of homework each night. It is often expected that even young children must read, practice sums, or research information at home. More and more "homework helper" websites let students ask an expert to find any information they need.

Some people argue that homework can cause stress in the home. Parents are not always able to help, and not all homes have the right books or computers. Even though many pupils and parents dislike horrid homework, it seems that it is here to stay!

Doing homework with the family can sometimes be fun.

How much homework do you have to do?

New ideas

New tools

In the 1960s many people warned that television was a bad idea. But TV has helped to bring education alive. In 1969 the programme *Sesame Street* began. Since then it has helped to educate millions of children. In the 1970s some people warned that electronic calculators would stop young people using their brains. Were they right?

The 1960s and 1970s were years of great change in schools. Many countries had new ideas about how to teach young people. Some schools gave children the choice to do almost whatever they liked, to let them express themselves freely. This was a great change from the past!

Many older students felt angry about events happening around them. In the 1960s some of the 70 million US teenagers and young adults wanted change. High schools and colleges became centres of unrest and arguments. In the 1970s students **protested** about things such as the Vietnam War, and they even caused riots.

Big Bird from *Sesame Street* has been educating children for over 30 years.

Word bank   **interactive** allowing two-way electronic communications
IT Information Technology

All change

The 1980s and 1990s saw the computer **revolution** move to schools. Today, **interactive** white boards are common in many classrooms, but even 10 years ago such technology was unheard of.

In the early 1980s less than half of all high schools in the United States and United Kingdom had computers for students to use. Within 10 years, nearly all classrooms had at least one computer, and most high schools had **IT** rooms or media centres with Internet access. Soon many schools had their own websites, and lessons were held with all students working on separate computers – each one with links to the Internet.

The early computers that were used in schools were big, slow, and did not do very much!

Changing laws

Through the 1960s and 1970s students were still **caned** in the United Kingdom and in some states in the United States. These places banned caning during the 1980s, and New Zealand banned it in 1990. Some states in the United States and areas of Australia have yet to ban **corporal punishment**.

revolution   sudden, extreme, or complete change

Where next?

Schools today have come a long way from the scary places they often were. At one time, nobody had even thought that learning could be fun. Many schools are now exciting places but, even so, some young people still have times when they do not want to go.

There will always be some young people who have a real fear of school. School **phobia** affects many pupils who become terrified even at the thought of school. Studies have shown that pupils learn best in lessons where jokes and humour are used. Happy schools are more likely to get happy results!

It is hoped that children all over the world will one day enjoy great schools.

Word bank   phobia   terrible fear of something

Making a difference

Schools, homework, teachers, and students have all had to change a great deal over the years. Today, more young people than ever before can read, write, and learn all kinds of skills that were beyond the wildest dreams of students in the past. Education has made a real difference to so many lives.

There are still countries where school is still beyond the dreams of many children. One of the biggest challenges in education in this century is for every child in the world to have the right to learn without fear, unfairness, or pain.

The schools of tomorrow?

Maybe all learning in the future will be by computer (below). Every lesson could be online, so all you would need would be a laptop or a mobile phone. Just think – you could be in the classroom without having to get out of bed!

Find out more

Bannned

These are some of the countries that have banned **corporal punishment** in schools over the last 250 years:

Year	Country
1783	Poland
1860	Italy
1881	France
1900	Japan
1917	Russia
1949	China
1970	Germany, Switerzerland
1982	Ireland
1986	UK
1990	New Zealand
1996	South Africa
1999	Zimbabwe
2000	Thailand,
2001	Kenya
2004	Canada

In most states in the US, corporal punishment is banned, but there are still some states that have not officially banned it.

Further reading

Cracking the Wall: The Struggles of the Little Rock Nine, (Lerner Classroom, 2003)

Life in the Past: Victorian Schools, Mandy Ross (Heinemann Library, 2005)

You Wouldn't Want to be a Victorian Schoolchild, John Malam (Hodder Children's Books, 2002)

Using the Internet

Explore the Internet to find out more about childhood education through time. You can use a search engine, such as **www.yahooligans.com**, and type in keywords such as:

- caning
- **dunce's** cap
- Little Rock High School

Search tips

There are billions of pages on the Internet so it can be difficult to find exactly what you are looking for.

These search tips will help you find useful websites more quickly:

- Know exactly what you want to find out about first.
- Use two to six keywords in a search, putting the most important words first.
- Be precise. Only use names of people, places, or things.

Roman numerals

Roman numbers were written as letters:

I = 1   L = 50   M = 1,000
V = 5   C =100
X = 10   D = 500

For example, 35 would be written as XXXV. Can you work out how to write 67 in Roman numerals? See the answer below.

School punishment

"For making fun of another pupil = a beating. For losing a school cap = a beating."

        – Hawkshead School, United Kingdom, 1585.

John Fitzpatrick

8 January, 1884: John Fitzpatrick was fighting on the street with James McNamara. Refused to stop when told to do so by some older pupils. He was struck on each hand three times with a ruler.

6 February, 1884: John Fitzpatrick has been repeating stories about boys in his class. He also has told me bare-faced lies about the matter. He was struck twice on each hand with a ruler.

        – From the school's "Black Book", New Rochelle, Westchester, New York, United States.

Growth in the United States

In 1870 only 2 percent of seventeen year olds graduated from high school. By 1900, however, 31 states required eight to fourteen year olds to attend school. As a result, by 1910, 72 percent of US children attended school, and half of the nation's children attended one-room schools.

A. The answer is LXVII.

Glossary

apprentice usually a young person learning a trade from a skilled worker

bishop leader of the Christian church

boarding school school where most of the pupils live during the school term

cane stick used to beat students as punishment

compulsory required by law to do something

convent house, school, or set of buildings run by nuns

corporal punishment punishment that hurts the body, such as hitting or whipping

discipline system of rules to control behaviour

disrupted thrown into disorder

dormitory large room where several people sleep in rows of beds

dripping solid fat from roasted meat, used in cooking or for food

dunce any pupil who did not work as quickly as the teacher wanted

evacuate remove people from a place of danger

exclude to keep out

governess woman who teaches and trains a child in a private home

hieroglyphics system of writing mainly in pictures, like scripts of the Ancient Egyptians

idle lazy and not active

immigrant person who comes to live permanently in a foreign country

Industrial Revolution time of great change and development in industry and work

infectious easily spread

inhabit when someone lives somewhere

interactive allowing two-way electronic communications

IT Information Technology

lashes beatings with a stick, whip, or cane

Latin language of ancient Rome and its empire

Middle Ages period of European history from about AD 500 to 1500

monastery place where a community of monks lives

monk man who gives up family life to join a religious group

nun woman who gives up family life to join a religious group

orphan young person whose parents have died

peasant poor person or farm worker

petticoat skirt or slip worn under a dress or outer skirt

philosophy study of ideas, meaning, truth, right and wrong

phobia terrible fear of something

protest display of unwillingness or disapproval

quill pen made from a feather

refugee person who flees to safety in another country, usually because of war or famine

revolution sudden, extreme, or complete change

Roman numerals ancient Roman way of writing numbers using letters

rural country areas away from towns and cities

satellite artificial body launched into orbit in space from Earth to collect information

scholar someone who attends a school or studies under a teacher

scribe person who studies, writes, or copies scripts

scroll roll of material that has been prepared as a writing surface

segregation separating one race, class, or group from another

slum city area with dirty run-down housing, and poor living conditions

taxes charges set by governments to pay for public services

UNESCO United Nations Educational, Scientific, and Cultural Organization

university place for learning different subjects, passing exams, and gaining qualifications

vicious dangerous or showing hateful feelings

Index